How to Start a Ranch

Be in Control of When and How You Work and Live out Your Passion

Weston Young

Table of Contents

Chapter 1: The Benefits of Starting a Ranch............................5
Chapter 2: Startup Costs for a Ranch..10
Chapter 3: How to Properly Set Up Your Ranching Business..24
Chapter 4: Basics of Raising Cows...33
Chapter 5: Assimilating Bulls In With the Cows......................41
Chapter 6: How to Move and Sell Beef Cattle..........................49
Chapter 7: Common Mistakes Even Experienced Ranchers Make that Can Run You Out of Business.................................55

☐ Copyright 2019 by Weston Young - All rights reserved.

This content is provided with the sole purpose of providing relevant information on a specific topic for which every reasonable effort has been made to ensure that it is both accurate and reasonable.

Nevertheless, by purchasing this content you consent to the fact that the author, as well as the publisher, are in no way experts on the topics contained herein, regardless of any claims as such that may be made within. As such, any suggestions or recommendations that are made within are done so purely for entertainment value. It is recommended that you always consult a professional prior to undertaking any of the advice or techniques discussed within.

This is a legally binding declaration that is considered both valid and fair by both the Committee of Publishers Association and the American Bar Association and should be considered as legally binding within the United States.

The reproduction, transmission, and duplication of any of the content found herein, including any specific or extended information will be done as an illegal act regardless of the end form the information ultimately takes. This includes copied versions of the work physical, digital and audio unless express consent of the Publisher is provided beforehand. Any additional rights reserved.

Furthermore, the information that can be found within the pages described forthwith shall be considered both accurate and truthful when it comes to the recounting of facts.

As such, any use, correct or incorrect, of the provided information will render the Publisher free of responsibility as to the actions taken outside of their direct purview.

Regardless, there are zero scenarios where the original author or the Publisher can be deemed liable in any fashion for any damages or hardships that may result from any of the information discussed herein.

Additionally, the information in the following pages is intended only for informational purposes and should thus be thought of as universal. As befitting its nature, it is presented without assurance regarding its prolonged validity or interim quality. Trademarks that are mentioned are done without written consent and can in no way be considered an endorsement from the trademark holder.

Chapter 1: The Benefits of Starting a Ranch

Ranching is known to have originated from Spain in the medieval times. The practice was common amongst noble families. They acquired huge pieces of land so that they could be able to herd cows and sheep in large fields. As time went by it was no longer a part-time hobby, those who practiced ranching wanted to earn an income from it.

In the modern age, ranching is both a hobby and a source of income for many. However, wouldn't it be great to do something that you are passionate about and still earn from it?

Aside from making money from ranching, there are many ways that you can benefit from the practice. If you are looking for reasons why you should start a ranch, here are some of the benefits that you can expect to gain from ranching.

You get to be in control of your working hours

Like any other self-employment opportunity, you will be able to set up your own time. A lot of people get tired when they have to follow a 9 to 5 job routine all day, every day, however, being a rancher will give you control over your working hours.

You get to choose how many hours you are going to work and your schedule is flexible and adjustable. It does not mean that you do not have to work or do much, but it is much more fulfilling to be your own boss and to have a say over the work hours and how much time you will need to allocate to your business every day.

When you have control over your own schedule you will be able to allocate more time to your family or to other projects that need your attention. You will have time to carry out your day to day activities.

It is therapeutic

According to research, one way of managing stress and depression is by engaging in a hobby as well as learning new things. Ranching can be enjoyable and fun and so it can act as a hobby.

Even if you do not have experience working on a ranch or you have not been anywhere near one, you can carry out your research and learn more about it. How does this end up being therapy for your mind?

Well think of it this way, the more time that you put into learning something new and engaging, the less time that your mind spends getting stressed or harboring on negative thoughts.

Due to the activities that you will need to carry out on the ranch such as taking care of the animals, you will be able to keep busy.

You will get to work with animals

You will find different types of animals in a ranch, which include and are not limited to; horses, cows, sheep, chickens, and pigs.

If you are an animal lover, this is an opportunity of a lifetime, since you will get to spend your time working closely with these animals, taking care of them, feeding them, and learning more about them.

Carry out research on the animals that you plan to house in your ranch. Learn their feeding patterns, diseases that are likely to affect them, medicines that they need, and care during pregnancy among other things.

Attend seminars and workshops on the subject, so that you are well informed and educated on all these matters.

If you have kids, they will get to learn how to properly take care of the animals at the farm and they will learn to value and respect animals as well.

You will get to earn an income from doing what you love

At the end of it all, earning money is still one of the main agenda's as you are starting a ranch. You want to follow your dream, and make sure that you earn money from it.

You will need to formulate a plan and carry out market research so you can understand beforehand how much money you intend to make. Doing this is probably the least amount of fun of this whole experience, yet that does not mean that it isn't critically important.

However, if you are in love with hard work it will not be exhausting for you. You will need to ask yourself several questions.

Which type of animals do you intend to keep on your ranch? Why and what profit do you intend to make? Carry out market research and make well-informed decisions.

Not many people get to earn from their hobbies and their passion, if you get to experience this, then you are one of the lucky ones.

You should also evaluate the reasons that you have for starting your ranch, and where you see the ranch in a few years.

Which direction do you want to take? Do you only want to reach the local market or do you want it to be a bigger platform?

Is it a full-time source of income or do you want it to remain as a part-time hustle? Whatever the choice you make, it will end up determining how much work you need to put into it.

You can grow your own vegetables

Vegetables which are fresh from the farm are healthier and tastier compared to those from the grocery store. You can set aside a small part in your ranch and opt to plant vegetables and fruits.

Buy seeds of what you want to plant in your farm so you can enjoy salads and healthy meals. There are a lot of chemicals being used in plants. However, not all of the chemicals that are commonly used today are necessary.

Sadly, some of these chemicals can promote cancer and they bring about other harmful effects to your body. The good news is that by planting your own vegetables in your ranch, you will be able to control and regulate the chemicals that you use.

You get to be away from all the noise and air pollution

Not everyone loves the busy and congested life of the city. Sometimes it can be so noisy, stuffy and there are all kinds of fumes being emitted.

Life in a country setting is much more relaxing and calming. People are able to move around, take long walks, there is a bigger and safer playground for kids, and it is quiet.

You will get to be away from the hustle and bustle in the city and start living in a serene environment.

Starting a ranch is not complicated even if you have not had experience before or taken up a course to guide you. There are a lot of resources online that you can go through.

If you need a reason to start a ranch, some of the benefits that have been mentioned above are reason enough to get you started on your journey into becoming a rancher.

There are a lot of benefits and there are also negatives just like in any other venture that you will ever start, but if the benefits outweigh the negatives you should get started on this amazing journey.

Chapter 2: Startup Costs for a Ranch

Owning a ranch sounds great. However, this is an investment on your part that is meant to generate income for you.

As with any other investment you can think of, you have to incur some costs. Of course, if you manage your ranch well, your investment will pay off and you will enjoy all the benefits stated in the previous chapter.

Here we are going to look at the various expenses one can expect to incur when starting their own ranch. They may seem basic and obvious, but they collectively contribute greatly to the successful setup of a ranch.

Land

If you are setting up a ranch, you definitely need land. And not just any land, but a large piece of land.

If you happen to have a large piece of land, setting up the ranch will be much cheaper for you. If you don't, you need to do some scouting and identify a piece of land that is large enough to comfortably accommodate your animals.

Given you are setting up a ranch, it is advisable to get land in the rural area. It is in these rural areas that you are going to find extensive pieces of land. And compared to urban areas, land in rural areas is much cheaper.

The size of land you will need for your ranch is dependent on the number of cattle you are planning to hold in your ranch. Of course, the bigger the piece of land the better. But if you have limited resources, you should consider a minimum of 30 acres per cow.

That is the recommended cow to land ratio. Therefore, to know the amount of land you will need to set up a ranch that properly accommodates all your cattle, multiply the number of cattle you have or are planning to purchase by the minimum recommended size of land per cow.

The cost of land varies depending on the location and the quality of the land. You should expect to spend anywhere between $3000 and $4000 per acre.

The cost per acre has been steadily rising over the years. Therefore, you can expect the figures to go up over the next few years as well.

Acquiring the Best Piece of Land for Your Ranch

The first step when looking to purchase a piece of land is to identify your goal. In this case, you already know what you want, and that is to set up a ranch. So what follows is now doing the dirty work.

You need to dive in and do some deep research to identify the best land to acquire for your ranch. Once you have settled on the state, go to the internet and find all the information on land brokerages that service your areas of interest.

Download as many brochures as possible. Also, if you can get more information from magazines and newspapers, get them. People can also provide you with invaluable information. If you know people who might help you identify the best piece of land, reach out to them.
The aim is to have all the options before you to make the most informed decision. You, however, should be careful with your sources of information. Be careful to only select those resources that offer credible information.

Now, start to organize all the resources you have collected by location, the price and the features on the property. Note down the listings that interest you.

Keep track of those that offer the most value to you and that is comparatively cheaper.

When comparing land, you should be wary of amateur experts who give biased advice. In fact, the rule of thumb is for you to focus on what you want and not what the so-called experts glorify. What they like may not be what you like.

For a ranch, some features will need to be carefully considered since this is a space you want to keep your cows in, and your cows will be what makes you profit. When trimming your options, consider the size of the land.

Is it able to comfortably accommodate all your cattle without them having to "fight" for the available resources? Does the piece of land have access to a water source for your animals? Are there enough pastures, etc.?

This stage of doing research can be quite scary and overwhelming. Don't let that stop you. This gives you more knowledge of the things you need to know that will help you get the most value for your money.

Work with a broker

Purchasing land to set up a ranch is in no way similar to buying a house. The process is more complex.

If you are knowledgeable of the process, you can handle the acquisition by yourself. But if you have little or no knowledge like most people, then the best way to go about acquiring land for a ranch is through a broker. And not just any broker.

You should find yourself a knowledgeable broker who knows the process and is able to negotiate the best deal for you.

An ideal broker is one you like, one who is knowledgeable, one who is trustworthy and one who understands and has experience in the business of ranching.

With the right broker, what remains is now finalizing the process and actually acquiring the land. Needless to say, by this stage, you should have already determined the size of land you will require.

The cash required to complete the purchase should also be ready for the process to be smooth.

You have to conduct the customary due diligence of the piece of land you want to purchase. This should take you anywhere between one to two months.

This is the time where you get to research the land and ensure what has been negotiated for purchase is what you're getting. Only proceed with the deal if everything checks out.

An important step that should not be skipped in the acquisition process is the physical inspection of the piece of land. Check to ensure that the land actually hosts all the features in its description.

The information unearthed during the due diligence process can be important in renegotiating your purchase. Also, if the land you inspect proves not to be as favorable to purchase as it seemed before, you can explore other options.

If everything checks out, you can now consider bringing in a good ranch transaction attorney to help formally finalize the purchase.

Ensure you obtain all the necessary documents that prove you are now the new and legitimate owner of the ranch.
At this stage, you can now consider fencing your ranch and bringing in your cattle.

Fencing

Fencing is crucial for a ranch if you want it to operate at an optimum level. A solid fence acts as a barrier that controls the movement of your cattle within the ranch. Other benefits of fencing include:

- **Providing safety for your animals**

    You can only get value from your animals if they are safe. Fencing your ranch goes a long way in ensuring that your cattle are safe. Fencing helps to prevent your cattle from wandering off to other farms and getting lost. Additionally, a fence helps keep predators away.

- **Makes stock breeding easy**

    With the movement of your livestock controlled by the fences, it becomes much easier for you to manage stock breeding hence increasing the value of your livestock.

- **Fencing makes it easier to manage a pasture**

    Fencing makes it easier for you to control how your livestock graze.

    By establishing a well-planned fence, you allow your animals to graze quality pasture without straining certain defined sections of the ranch while neglecting others.

- **Creates order**

    While you will be running the ranch to make money, you should not neglect order and aesthetic appeal.

    Proper fencing ensures that your ranch looks functional and pleasing. The visual attractiveness of your ranch makes it even more valuable and easy to run.

- **Increases the value of the ranch**

A fence also increases the resale value of the ranch. If you consider reselling the land in the future, you can be sure to have higher chances of getting a prospective buyer much faster just because the ranch is well fenced.

- **Prevent the spread of pests and diseases**

  Fencing is crucial in keeping away pests and diseases, especially by limiting the interactions between the animals in your ranch and those from other farms. Also, in case some of your livestock have been infected, it is much easier to keep them isolated.

There are many more benefits that come with fencing. These are just a fraction.

But for you to enjoy these benefits, you have to incur additional costs. Fencing costs about $2 per unit foot.

The perimeter length of your ranch together with the defined sections you want to add within the camp will determine how much money you will spend on fencing.

If you sum up the amount of money you have to spend to purchase the ranch and the amount you need for fencing, the numbers appear to be quite large.

While the cost of land is always high, you can save some good amount of cash buying land that is already fenced off.

This will help you save some money by avoiding the fencing costs you would have incurred.

Feed for Animals

Other than the natural pastures, you need to provide your livestock with quality animal feed. Natural pastures are good.

But if you want your animals to reach their optimal production capacity, you need to provide them with quality animal feeds that offer balanced nutrition for the livestock.

This means you will need to do some research and identify the best animal feed supplier near the location of your ranch. The best feed program is that which:

- **Has been manufactured with a science-based nutritional philosophy**

    There should be a deep understanding of animal nutrition. The feeds provided should be manufactured according to the nutritional requirement guidelines by the NRV.

    The feed ratios should be formulated by experts for optimal performance of your commercial livestock.

- **The feeds have ingredients of top quality**

    The ingredients used in making the feeds should be clean, safe, have a consistent appearance and be formulated and manufactured rigorously.

To get the best from your livestock, you need to offer them the best. This means that the feeds you provide them have to be of high quality.

Identify the most trustworthy animal feed supplier near your location and have them deliver animal feed to your ranch for your animals.

Animal care

For your ranch establishment to be fruitful, a lot of effort has to be invested in ensuring that the welfare of the animals is well taken care of.

The safety, health and the comforts of the animals should be put ahead of everything else.

Animal Safety

There are so many ways of defining animal safety. Basically, it is ensuring that your livestock is not harmed in any way.

One of the main safety features on a farm is the fence that was mentioned earlier. A solid fence helps keep your livestock confined and protected from any external predators.

Other than the fence, it is important to ensure that the ranch has well-defined structures where the animals sleep and where they feed. These places should have enough lighting and adequate security to keep an eye on them.

Part of making the safety of your livestock a priority is ensuring that their food is safe.

Your feed supplier should be able to supply you with fresh and highly nutritious feeds that only contribute to the improvement of the health and productivity of your livestock.

Animal Health

Another important consideration when running a ranch is monitoring the health of your livestock. If keen attention is not directed towards ensuring that your livestock is healthy, then you should be ready to watch all your investment crumble to the ground.

Healthy animals feed well. This means that the ranch has to have enough pasture for all your cattle.

This is something you need to consider before you purchase the ranch. Ensure that the pastures are taken care of properly. Adopt an effective method of grazing that ensures the pastures are properly utilized.

Supplement the pastures with high-quality animal feeds. The animal feeds should have a balanced nutrition content to cater to all the nutritional needs of your livestock.

In fact, you should consider hiring the services of an animal nutritionist. They can offer you the best advice on the best feed to get your livestock. They can help you draft a good feeding program for your livestock.

Other than nutritious feed, ensure that your animals have access to clean and safe drinking water.

Another aspect to consider with regards to the health of your animals is the cleanliness of their housing. It is important to ensure that the places your animals sleep are kept as clean as possible.

Just as in humans, cleanliness helps keep away pests and diseases. An unclean area provides good grounds for bacteria and other infectious organisms to thrive.

If your animals end up getting sick, then they will not have anything to offer you and will be of no value to you. As such, it is important to tidy up the places where your animals eat and sleep.

Vaccination helps protect your livestock against diseases. That is why if you are considering establishing a ranch, you should have a veterinary officer on speed dial.

You will have to ensure that all the animals in the ranch have been vaccinated against all possible diseases. This will help prevent and reduce cases of disease outbreaks in your ranch.

You also have to consider ways of ensuring that your sick animals receive proper care and treatment. This means that you have to plan the ranch in such a way that there are defined sections where the sick animals can be kept and given special attention until they have fully recovered.

These are, basically, the main areas that you have to consider when thinking about animal care for your livestock.

Animal Comfort

Your livestock should be comfortable in your ranch. This means that they should have sufficient space to move around and a clean and comfortable space for them to sleep.

If you think about it, the safety and the health of your livestock, also, contributes to the comfort of your livestock.

Ranch Insurance

If you run a ranch, then you will need ranch insurance. Ranch insurance is almost similar to farm insurance only that it focuses on livestock.

The aim of the cover is to protect the ranch against unexpected damage or loss.

What ranch insurance covers

Most ranches include a home. This makes their coverage pretty unique.

Most ranch insurance covers both the home and the business— since ranches are businesses of course. The covers offered by ranch insurance basically include the following:

- **Dwelling coverage**

Dwelling coverage protects your home in the ranch in the event of damage caused by a catastrophic weather condition such as a wildfire or a tornado. It, also, covers theft and vandalism.

- **Liability coverage**

This type of coverage shields your ranch from big liability claims like damage to someone else's property, injury to the body, medical expenses or huge legal defense bills.

Other than these, you can get more coverage depending on the goals you have set and the unique situations you find yourself in. Some of these coverages worth considering include:

- **Livestock coverage**

A livestock cover helps protect your livestock in the event of a catastrophic occurrence that leads to their death. In fact, you can even purchase animal mortality insurance.

- **Equipment coverage**

Equipment coverage protects the equipment in your ranch. Having this cover makes it easier to have them replaced in the event of an accident that leads to damage.

- **Outbuilding/Barn coverage**

Protect other structures in your ranch like your warehouses. Ranching is a business and just like any other business, there are huge risks involved.

For that reason, special insurance covers that cover the business side of a ranch also exist. They include:

- **Loss of Business income cover**

In the event that a business interruption occurs or you lost some income due to a unique occurrence, this cover protects you by ensuring you recover all the lost income.

- **Commercial vehicle cover**

Protects your transport trucks, trailers and big rigs that you use to run your ranch business.

- **Professional liability coverage**

This cover helps protect you in the event that you end up making an operational mistake that lead other people to incur financial losses.

- **Workers' compensation cover**

This cover protects your employees and ranch workers from injury, illness or any accident that occurs while carrying out their duties on the ranch.

If you are setting up a ranch, you have the option to purchase a ranch insurance cover. The rewards of running a ranch are great.

But with them come even greater risks. Insurance covers can help you get back on your feet easily in the event that you find yourself in a disaster—whether operational or natural.

Ranch Insurance Cost

The policy premiums you will be required to pay will be determined by how big your ranch is and the kind of property you are insuring. The higher the property value is, the more the premiums you have to pay.

The factors that determine the amount you will have to pay for your ranch insurance include:

- The size and the use of your property
- The location of your ranch
- Your revenue
- Your equipment inventory
- Your animal inventory
- Proximity to a fire hydrant

There may be more information required depending on your insurance service provider, but those are some of the basics.

Financing a Ranch

There are so many things that one requires to run a ranch. And they all require one to produce money.

Just setting up the ranch will take you back hundreds of thousands of dollars. Therefore, you have to explore all the possible avenues of getting money.

The financing options available

- **Use your savings or inheritance as your starting capital**

If you are lucky to have saved enough money from your current job or if you have some trust fund from your parents or grandparents, then you can use that to fund your ranch investment without having to go into debt.

- **Get a loan**

Another option you can explore to get money for your ranch business is acquiring a loan. You can then use the profits you make from your ranch to repay the loan.

You, however, should note that you have to have an impressive credit score to qualify for a large loan size. Also, you should be able to prove that you are able to repay the loan once your ranch is operational.

- **Get a partner and invest together**

You can, also, get a partner who is interested in the ranching business and set up the ranch together. This will require that you draft a formal agreement on how you are both going to run the ranch.

A partnership means you will have to share the responsibilities, the risks and even the profits.

While sharing the profits may not seem all that glossy, bringing in a partner can help ease the burden off your shoulders by helping you avoid excessive debt or having to give up some of your assets to finance your investment.

Chapter 3: How to Properly Set Up Your Ranching Business

Running a ranch is running a business. While you may establish a home in your ranch, the ranch is still a business since you are running it for purposes of generating profits and making an income out of it.

As such, you are required to follow the relevant procedures just as you would when starting up any other business.

Business Plan

The first thing to do is to come up with a business plan. A business plan helps define the anatomy of your business.

It helps show how the ranch will run and how the various elements will collaborate to make the business profitable.

The important components to include in your business plan for your ranch include:

1. Land Resource Management

The land and the livestock are what will make you money. As such, your business plans should include a section that describes the land resources that will be crucial in the management of the ranch.

Include maps if they are available. Since you will be dealing with pasture and livestock, you should include a section that describes your grazing management plan in detail.

2. Equipment and livestock management

Basically, you will be using your animal resources and your equipment resources to convert the land resources into profit. In this section of the business plan, provide an inventory of all the equipment to be used on the farm.

With the inventory should, also, come defined maintenance plans and the replacement criteria.

You should provide an inventory of your livestock. Be sure to include details such as the breeding plans, genetics, the nutrition plans, health plans and any other protocols that will affect how the animals in the ranch are handled.

3. Human resources

Human resources are critical in successfully running a ranch. If you want to keep your employees, you need to establish strong and well-defined human resource policies for your ranch workers.

These are the people who will be managing the daily activities of the ranch.

This section of the business plan should detail the various personnel that will facilitate the smooth operations of the ranch and the specific roles they will be playing.

4. Market Plans

For your ranch to make you money, you must deliver something to the market. In the market plan section, identify the products and services from your ranch that you would like to sell.

It should not be complicated but you can build on your initial market plan as time progresses.

5. Financial section

This is the section where you display how your numbers will work. This is the section to include your statements, balance sheets, cash flows for the ranch and financial risk management plans.

This is a very key section as it provides a clear picture of how the numbers work in your ranch. Unlike most of the other parts of the business plan, the financial section needs to be updated regularly if you want your ranch to be profitable.

The bottom line is if you are running a ranch, you are running a business. And running a business requires that you have a business plan.

The Best Business Entity for your Ranch

When it comes to running a ranch, you're probably the only person who knows exactly how it operates. You know the number of acres of the ranch and have knowledge of all the items in the ranch's inventory.

With this vast knowledge and understanding of your ranch, creating a business entity only brings more benefits to your ranch operations.

Ranching, being an agricultural activity, can be categorized as a sole proprietorship, a corporation, a partnership or a limited liability company. Most ranch owners register their business as a sole proprietorship.

That said, each of the stated business entities come with their own share of pros and cons. It is upon you to weigh them and know which one best applies to you and your ranch business.

Sole Proprietorships

Just as the name hints, in a sole proprietorship, you are the owner of the ranch and its operator. All the profits come to you and you are the one in charge of handling all the tax liabilities.

All the money that is made through the business is yours. It is that simple.

The downside of a sole proprietorship is that there is no boundary that is established between you and your business. What this means is that if there are any liabilities or debts, they will be charged on you personally.

Therefore, any loans or credits that have been taken on for purposes of running the ranch are assumed to be your personal loans. Also, the actions of your employees are yours to bear as well.

Partnership

Partnerships happen when more than one party join together to contribute to the running of the business. While it is highly recommended, you are not legally required to have an agreement written out with your partner.

You, however, need to register your partnership.

Partnerships are great. Other than being inexpensive, they bring together different skills and expertise hence making it possible to make the ranch at its optimum capacity easily.

But the downside is that there is a huge risk of disagreements that may disrupt the operations of the ranch.

The best kind of partners are those who are willing to compromise and listen to the other partners.

Corporations

Corporations are on their own. The profits they get are on their own and they account for their liabilities.

Here, the ranch is treated as a company and the owners have shares in the company.

One of the major disadvantages of running a ranch as a corporation is that it requires a lot of time and comes with loads of paperwork.

Limited Liability Company (LLC)

A Limited Liability Company is somewhat a blend of a sole proprietorship, partnership, and a corporation.

One of its greatest advantages is that it offers liability protection just like in a corporation, while at the same time exercising a number of the operational benefits that come with partnerships and a sole proprietorship.

A Limited Liability Company can be structured in a variety of ways to conform to the operational needs of your ranch.

Registering your Business Name

All businesses need to have a business name for them to operate. Given you will be operating your ranch for the purpose of making profits; you will need to give it a name.

You need to spend time and pick the best name for your ranch. The reason being is that the ranch is your business and the name you give it will be associated with your brand.

As such, you need to find a name that complements the image of your brand as you want it to be seen.

Other than the name complementing your brand, it has to be unique. This means that no other business should bear a similar name.

The registration of businesses is usually done at the office of the secretary of state. Before your business name is approved, your Secretary of State will cross check with the other business names in the state to ensure the name has not been taken.

If there are no conflicts, then the name can be registered.

It is important to note that the business name you choose can be registered with a fictitious name or a trading name.

The difference between the two is that while a fictitious name does not necessarily have to be distinguishable and is not protected from being used by other businesses, a trading name must be distinguishable.

With a fictitious name, you do not gain exclusive rights to the name.

Registering a business name should take you back about $50. You can find the registration forms at your Secretary of State's website.

Getting a Tax ID Number for your Ranch Business

After you have had your business name registered, the next step is to obtain your business tax ID number, otherwise known as an Employee Identification Number. The Employee Identification Number is a unique number that allows the IRS to identify a business. You are required to provide all the tax forms and documents.

You can apply for a Tax ID Number via mail, phone or by fax. The most suitable and recommended method of filing your application is by making an online submission.

The application is pretty short and simple. In fact, you can get your Employee Identification Number immediately once you are done.

All you have to do is visit the IRS website and click on the "Begin Application" button that is located at the bottom of the page to get going. Once there, you will be required to provide answers to five short questions.

The first question asks you to select the EIN type you want to apply for—sole proprietorship, partnership, corporation, Limited Liability Company or estate. The questionnaire, also, asks for your official name and social security number to complete the application process.

Once you are done filling out the application, an Employee Identification Number will be generated by the system. You can commence using the number immediately.

The IRS will send you an official document to confirm that your application was successful and to confirm your EIN. With the tax ID number, you will now be able to employ workers in your ranch if you need to.

Aside from registering your business name and obtaining an Employee Identification Number, you also need to check the policies that govern your state and ensure that you obtain all the local permits and state permits that are required. The idea is to streamline your business to conform to all the requirements of the law.

The business licenses and permits can be obtained at your local county clerk's office. The application requires that you describe what your cattle ranch does and generally how it operates. You will be required to provide all the details regarding your ranch.

All you need to get this accomplished is to have your tax ID number and receipts indicating that you have paid the required processing fees. Once your application has been completed successfully, you will have to wait for several weeks, usually a month, for the licenses and permits to be provided.

If you are going to transport animals to and from another state, you will be required to apply for a federal license. You can apply for this through the Department of Agriculture's website.
The local permits differ from one place to another.

Getting an insurance cover for your ranch

An insurance cover is another important factor to consider adding before you begin running your camp. Getting a comprehensive insurance cover for your ranch ensures that you are insulated from loss in the event of an accident or if a calamity strikes.

Be sure to negotiate for the best deal from your insurance service provider. As you know, insurance companies are for profit and they always want to pay the least amount of money possible for compensation.

You, therefore, should consider sharpening your negotiation skills and get the best insurance package for your ranch.

Running the Ranch

With all the documents and permits in order, all that is left for you is to actually run the ranch and start making money. If you are someone who has some experience running a farm with animals, it can be easier for you to get going.

However, if you are someone who is not knowledgeable about livestock farming in a ranch, you may need to pause a little and get things in order first.

One of the best strategies to use is to get hooked to a small business organization to help you get started. You can learn from them on the most effective ways of running a ranch and how to best maximize the potential of your land.
Another important thing that any rancher should invest in is knowledge. This means you need to spend a good amount of your time reading books and blogs to get equipped with the best industry practices and to know of the recent developments in your location that may affect the operations of your ranch.

Getting the right manpower to run the daily operations of the ranch

For you to effectively manage the ranch, you will need to get knowledgeable manpower to help with the daily operations of the ranch. Your workers need to know how to handle livestock. They need to know when the animals are okay and when they are not. They need to know the best practices that will help the animals be at their best.

You should always draft formal employment letters for the people you employ. This will ensure that you get the best and the most out of them.

Get the best nutritionist and veterinary officer to watch the health and nutrition of your livestock. If possible, draft a contract with them to ensure that they offer your livestock the best care possible.

The process of setting up a ranch and making it operational is very daunting but has to be done with the uttermost keenness. Just one missing document could prove to be very costly to your business.

As such, you should always know what is required of you and all the steps you will have to go through before commencing the application process.

Chapter 4: Basics of Raising Cows

Raising cows or rather cattle is one of the most lucrative activities in agribusiness. There are many ways to raise cattle and they all come with their own degree of expenses.

In current times, there are both modern as well as traditional ways of raising cattle. How cows or cattle are brought up and nurtured does not only depend on the knowledge and skill of the farmer but also the animal's breed, type and class.

They all react differently to different weather conditions and have different feeding habits. Yes, you might think that all they do is eat grass and drink water, so how hard can it be?

But when we are looking at it from a ranch perspective, there are a lot of other factors that must be considered. The following are some of the things you'll want to consider as part of raising cattle:

Pasture Management

The first thing that comes to mind when planning a ranch is what will your animals feed on? They cannot just graze on barren land or seasonally grassed lands.

You have to know what they feed on as well as what their feeding schedule looks like. Cattle feed on a lot of things and most are essential for their well being and overall health. They feed on grass, silage, supplements, hay and grain. So a cocktail of a couple of them is what they should be fed on a daily basis.

The type of cattle that you're keeping will determine what amount of feed you provide and at what frequency. Dairy cattle tend to consume quite a lot in addition to specialized supplements because of the quality of milk they produce.

If you want top-notch creamy and thick milk you have to stay on top of their nutrition. Keeping beef cattle, on the other hand, is not quite as tedious as the previous type because they can survive and get fed on only grass and hay, it's as simple as that.

Regardless of the type of cattle you have, make sure that you go the extra mile in terms of food provision and the type of meals you provide.

In the case of your pasture, keep in mind the number of cattle you are keeping as well as the size of the land that you're using. Have an adequate and sensible stocking rate to prevent your land from being overgrazed which will leave it prone to erosion.

You should have a rotational method of grazing that is related to the number of cattle you have. This allows for proper grazing as well as ample time for the land to rejuvenate.

Health Program

You have to remember that these are animals that are vulnerable to weather elements and infections diseases from time to time. It's considered a normal part of ranching for your cattle to get sick from time-to-time.

Even with this being the case, how prepared are you in case of a break out of a disease that is out of the ordinary? A health program is very imperative especially if you're introducing new cattle with your existent cattle.
Your new visitors could be vectors of pest and diseases that could very easily spread and affect both your cattle and your wallet at the same time. A health program also comes in handy if your area is one where diseases tend to be prevalent whether they are out in the field or confined inside a barn.

The type of food or supplements that you provide for your cattle could be affecting them as well. So it's up to you to know which supplements goes well with which cattle.

You also need to know the supplements reactive qualities and a possible method of treatment in case over consumption happens.

Having health programs keeps you in check with your cattle as you'll always be on the lookout for symptoms and signs of altered behavior that is out of the norm. It's also not always about treating an infection but rather preventing it.

Before you set up your ranch make sure that your piece of land has been certified and passed through as safe from pests and other disease-causing elements.

For cattle, it's not all about vaccination or quarantine periods but keeping them on the safer route of prevention. This can be achieved by providing a feed that is rightfully adequate with the correct amount of nutrition as well as carrying out strict operational management protocols to keep their well being in balance.

As we all know, some things happen unexpectedly and accidents could happen at any moment. With this being the case, you should be well equipped and have specific items or tools in case of emergencies.

Bear in mind that the items you need will be dependent on the type of cattle you're going to own. It wouldn't be sensible to keep sheers if you're going to keep dairy cattle for example. In the long road, things don't always go as planned and at times some animals may not make it. Some cannot be completely cured and they may succumb to their conditions. You may be forced to euthanize the animal by yourself and yes it might sound heartless and gruesome but it may be the only chance you have of saving your other cattle from catching the disease.

In these cases it's best to use a method that will quickly take the animal out of its misery without feeling much pain. Some owners use a gun shooting the cow high in the center of the forehead, or you could have a vet euthanize the animal via injection.

Managing Silage, Crops, And Hay

Some ranchers prefer to produce their own feed where as others purchase it. If you are part of the first group, then this is an operation that you'll have to carry out keeping in mind your cattle type as well as the climatic seasons and conditions that surround you.

Depending on your cattle type, you may choose to feed your cattle in the conventional way, which is where your cattle graze all summer and are confined and fed during the winter.

However it is that you choose to feed your cattle, you must have a perfect grip on these operations. Doing so will give you the best possible chance of keeping your livestock well-fed and healthy.

For your feeding success, you need to keep in mind the right seeding and harvesting period. This will ensure that your feed is of the right quality as well as possessive of the right and matured vitamins and nutrients.

In the case of silage preparation, ensure that you harvest it at the right time. Over preparing or under-preparing detracts it of the qualities that need to be present, thus making it less nutritious than it is supposed to be.

As far as hay preparation is concerned, one needs to cut and level it at the required time, allowing it to dry during the preparation period, and then rake and bale it. Hay can be quite tricky since a single spark can cause your whole load to go up in flames.

So you need to make sure proper safety protocols are in place as well.

The equipment required for you to undertake in these operations have to be kept in good shape. It does not necessarily have to be brand new equipment, but rather it's how you maintain and take care of it.

This would include things such as regularly sharpening your cutting tools and greasing moving parts to prevent rusting. Also make sure that you clean your equipment after use and store it in proper and accessible places.

Any broken parts should be repaired or replaced immediately for your safety as well as to make sure that you're still able to get your work done on time.

How to identify injured or sick cattle

Cattle just like humans when in distress will give out signs and signals that they are not doing well. Accurately diagnosing cattle requires you to be alert at all times.

Some signs may be internal, which means the issue might persist until it is too late to save the animal. The early recognition of a sign that something is wrong is critically important.

This will allow you to be able to provide early treatment and medical attention for the sick animal as soon as possible if warranted. It also saves on extra expenditures that could have been incurred if the condition got out of hand and spread to other livestock.

 Taking care of illnesses as soon as possible can also prevent the cow from going through extra stress. Some common signs you want to be on the lookout for include:

Appetite

Just like with humans, when cattle are sick there appetite will go away. Cattle that used to be active and perceived as aggressive when it comes to their feeding habits will immediately be seen as dull and will hardly show up at the feeding trough.

The amount of food they intake as compared with their average food intake will be significantly less. If a cow suddenly stops eating that should definitely give you pause for concern. You can also compare its feeding habits to its herd mates and see if there's any missing links or irregularities.

Temperature

Animals get fevers too. In this case, when handling animals that you may suspect to be unwell, you can use a digital thermometer. In normal ranges, the constant for most herds are considered to be between 101 to 103 degrees.

Any recorded temperatures that are either above or below that range should be taken very seriously. The values might keep changing depending on the current season and on the climatic conditions that are present.

Something like heat stress during the summer time might alter temperatures as well. Considering that cattle aren't cheap, it is advised that you take to take a temperature reading of your cattle on a daily basis so you'll know if and when any irregularities occur.

Legs and hooves

Looking at a cow's hooves is an important thing to look at, yet many ranchers don't do this. Sometimes a cow's hooves could be injured by sharp objects or by things that get stuck in their hooves.

These little things that persist could resort to causing infections that may be septic. Observing how your cattle run, walk or even stand will tell you a lot about its health physically. Be sure to keep an eye out lesions and hoof warts.

Droppings/manure

Looking at the animals' droppings and making a comparison is important. This might be a comparison to its previous discharge or with other herd mates.

The animals' droppings will be a sign of what is going on internally. This could suggest an issue with the cow's digestive system.

Therefore be on the lookout for diarrhea or dry stool as signs that something could be wrong.

General appearance

Looking at the general appearance of your cattle is also an effective way to see if something is potentially wrong. The skin, eyes, and posture of the animal all mean something if closely looked at.

Is it panting excessively, is it dull, does it always want to sleep? These are all signs that something could be wrong.

You can also compare the animal's behavior to the behavior of the other cattle. It may appear sleepy or tired all of the time.

It may have also lost interest in previous activities that it used to do. In general, be on the lookout with a keen eye and you will be able to see a potential problem at hand and take care of it before it worsens.

Chapter 5: Assimilating Bulls In With the Cows

You can never get enough experience handling bulls and cattle. Animals are not scripted beings and can act any way that they choose to for any reason at all.

Even if you have an extensive line of expertise with cattle you're still prone to injuries and accidents around them. When handling these animals one has to keep their safety in mind as well as safety precautions for the animals.

Handling cattle that are heavier and bigger than you requires a specialized approach since it's quite easy for them to cause injuries thanks to their large size.

For one to handle the cattle effectively and safely, they first have to know their animal well. This is in terms of behaviors as well as characteristics during specific operations.

There are certain points you need to keep in mind when working with cattle. Following these pointers will help to keep you safe and minimize any potential accidents.

Therefore, when handling cattle one has to be keen on the following:

The Animal's Sight and Sounds

When you're around animals always keep in mind that they do not function the same as we do. Their senses of sight and hearing are not of the same degree as ours.

Cattle are known to possess a sharp sense of hearing which makes even the slightest of sounds seem exaggerated and loud to them.

What we might dismiss as a whisper or soft sound could be interpreted differently by the animal and therefore cause an unexpected change in their behavior.

They are animals and they therefore react differently to environmental stimuli than humans do.

Bulls, are known to be dominant and aggressive, therefore one should be even more cautious when working with bulls. This is because once they're scared they get an urge or tendency to fight.

While bulls will take this challenge head-on, cows are more of flight animals. This means that in case of a scare or fright cows will take off and run to whichever direction they'll see as a safe haven.

This could be extremely dangerous if a whole herd was running towards you. You can imagine just how dangerous a stampede of scared animals can be.

Cattle are also known to have a bad depth perception which in turn makes them act scared in dark places. The amount of light that is in an area affects them and how they conduct themselves.

Also, one has to be keen on an animal's blind spot as well as flight zones. When a cow is looking straight ahead, it can not see it's rear.

Therefore, you must be careful if you're behind the cow because you might get kicked without the cow even realizing that you were behind it.

Handling Bulls

Bulls by their very nature can tend to be aggressive. They are known to have injured and even killed people over the years on fields and ranches.

Bulls can either be kept for breeding or used just for beef purposes. The aggressiveness of a bull is also depend on what breed it is.

With this being the case, all of the bulls' pens should have special markings that will alert anyone who wishes to carry out any activities with the bulls to be mindful of how to handle that specific animal.

Before carrying out any operations or activities, you must first locate the bull. This is to help keep you alert so that the bull can not surprise you.

Another important thing is to know where all of the exits are. This will help you know the fastest route to an exit in case of a confrontation or charge.

Having all your bulls wear bells is an effective method of identifying them even in a large herd. Whenever you find yourself in a situation where the bull gets aggressive, stop anything that you could be doing, and get to a safe place.

Make sure that you conduct yourself in a calm manner so that you don't scare the animals, and also make sure that you keep your bull in sight. Most of the time before a bull attacks; it puts its head down or even arches its back.

When handling these animals, at times you cannot carry out certain tasks alone. This means that if you are shorthanded, your chances of getting hurt are going to be higher.

When you are amongst the herd, make sure that you are in an open place outside of the herd. Never get yourself caught in the middle amongst them.

Don't trust them that much, anything could trigger them and their immediate reflex response could result in your death or injury. Also as you have established your ranch, make sure that your gates, as well as the doors, are not in a position to easily pin you.

As you build your ranch, make sure that you have a well thought-out design that will be easily accessible and spacious enough for both you and your cattle.

When handling cattle keep in mind that they don't forget traumatic experiences easily. If something happened to the animal at a specific section of the ranch, it may be afraid or hesitant to even go there again.

This means that if you scared it or showed aggression towards it, it may forever see you in a bad light. Animals just like humans have feelings and they have emotions as well.

The way you treat them will be reflective of how they will treat or conduct themselves around you.

In general, cattle like to have a specific routine that they can live by. This means that as part of your operation management, you should have in place routines that are to be followed at specific times.

This will ensure that your entire workforce is well conversant with the timeline of procedures that are to be carried out in order to keep the animals comfortable.

Once an animal is more relaxed and used to a specific routine, it will be much easier to manage and control.

Breeding

Cattle breeding season may solely depend on the owner if the owner is using the control method, but if it's natural, then breeding will mostly occur around spring. Many producers however oft for the same, springtime.

This because they like taking full advantage of the lush pastures and grasses that grew during that period. Whichever mode of breeding the rancher may decide on, it is advised that the bull should be given time to run with the cows for approximately 60-90 days.

This method gives you the chance to feed all your cattle at once without having to go around secluding and handling both parties at the different times. This helps cut down on the labor as well as expenses that may be incurred during this period.

When breeding your heard, you first have to know how many bulls and cows are present and able to breed. And by able, I'm referring to the cattle that are both strong and healthy and can produce viable offspring.

So you have to identify which bulls and cows will breed. An individual mature bull can service up to thirty cows on average.

In the case of yearling bulls, you can lower the number to twenty. Make sure that you prepare your cattle to be able to breed by ensuring that they're physically able and aren't too thin or too fat.

As far as breeding methods are concerned, artificial insemination is an effective way to go about it. This is because the rancher can control the breeding as well as use a high-quality bull that could not be afforded otherwise to service their cows.

This method keeps the rancher ahead of time in the sense that he will be able to know when calving will occur and plan out the breeding period appropriately. However, ranchers are advised to have back up cows just in case the artificial insemination was not a success.

Whether the owner opts for the natural or artificial insemination method, they can still depend on the performance data of an animal to know which bulls are up to the task to mate with specific cows.

This will also help you be able to project what kind of offspring to expect in terms of breed type, weight or other vital qualities. Some people choose to leave their animals to breed without any sort of timeline, as in they will try to breed year round.

This requires nature's call on the animals to mate.

This kind of breeding, however, comes with its own set of advantages and disadvantages as well. Some of the advantages include:

- Cows will produce milk all throughout the year. This kind of milk apart from breastfeeding calves can be consumed in households.
- Keeping the bull in the herd as it wanders with the others helps conduct simpler bull management. This is because you are in an open space and it is much easier to control the bull when it isn't confined.
- A bull will notice heat signs in a cow while out in the herd much easier than ranchers sometimes will. Once a cow comes into heat, it is immediately serviced by the reigning bull.
- It is much easier to monitor the animals' conception rates as well as know which cow has not conceived and why.

This method also comes with its own set of disadvantages and they include the following:

- You'll need adequate pasture space all throughout the year if you would want good conception rates. This means that you need to have an endless supply of feed for the heavy cows, calving cows as well as the bulls. You also have to keep in mind that they all eat at different rates depending on what season they are in.

- Health practices are supposed to be done all year round. If the animals were restrained in barns or pens, vaccinations and other management operations would be easier to complete. However, since they are in a field, they are constantly exposed to various disease-causing organisms, leaving them vulnerable to fall ill at any time.

- You require more bulls if you have a large herd with the majority of that herd being cows. During the breeding season, some cows may miss the chance to breed due to lack of time or there not being enough bulls in the herd.

- If the rancher opts for the artificial insemination method of breeding, then they'd have to search the entire herd for a cow that could be in heat. This could definitely be seen as a tedious task that may not be the best use of your time.

- Keeping the bulls together mixed in with the herd means that over time only one bull will end up servicing the cows. This is because bulls fight for dominance and the most dominant bull will take rein and service all the cows.

Aside from trying to breed year-round, there is also seasonal breading. This is a method that has been used with the aim of reducing the lactation period during the dry season.

This helps to preserve the animal's body condition as well as support the egg's development and the ovarian function. Short seasonal breeding means that there will be little expenditure in terms of supplements and feed provisions.

This is because there will be little to no lactations during the dry season. In this same way, it helps to identify reproductive diseases as well as making bull testing much more efficient.

There are factors that determine the time that should be considered for the ideal mating season. Some of them include:

- The nutritional requirements of the breeder-Breeders are supposed to be supplied with highly nutritious feeds that are essential during this period.

- The environmental factor- The harshness of the surroundings may affect breeding since the nutritional content of the feed may not be up to par. Good nutritional content will help the cows recover their ovarian function in a good amount of time.

- Having your bull out- Getting your bull out should not be difficult but if there is even a slight chance that having the bull out at a desired time could cause an issue, then it is advised to start the mating season much earlier.

- Marketing policies- Marketing an empty cow earlier during the year is a tactic used to take full advantage of the best prices as well as generate a good cash flow.

Chapter 6: How to Move and Sell Beef Cattle

There are different breeds of cattle and being in the business, you will need to carry out your research so you can find out how many breeds of cattle you want to own.

Some of the different kinds of cattle include the following; the Texas longhorn which is easily identifiable due to its long horns, Brahman, Hereford, Brangus, Beef master, and Angus among others.

Each breed has a different market value so you'll definitely want to take that into consideration when deciding what you want to own.

Even before you can get to the stage of moving and selling your cattle, you will need to take good care of them so you can be able to reap good profits. You will need to understand that there are different phases of beef farming.

For instance, in a herd of 50 cows, a farmer is likely to purchase 2 bulls. In a one year period, you can expect roughly 90% of the cows to conceive.

Once those cows have given birth, they are then sold to another farmer who will use a specialized feed so they can gain more weight. After the cattle have grown, they are then sold so they can be slaughtered for beef.

How do you take proper care of the beef cattle that you are going to sell?

Taking care of your cattle does not just involve taking care of their health. Here are some ways that you can ensure that your cattle are well taken care of:

Ensure that you give your cattle an environment that is free from stress

Interact with your cattle in a calm manner to avoid scaring them. Stress will bring with it various diseases in animals.

In fact, every living being when subjected to stress is unable to live a healthy life. Take your time to create a comfortable atmosphere for your herd.

How are your cattle feeding?

You can tell if your cattle are feeding well just by looking at them. When they are well fed, their general appearance is healthy and they tend to have a round stomach.

Also look out for their behavior patterns. For instance, are they missing meals?

Healthy cattle always come out to feed during meal times, and you can therefore keep track of this quite easily if you are feeding them hay. Additionally look out for their activity levels.

Certain changes in behavior may mean that they might be sick and they may need medical attention.

Make sure that they all stay up-to-date with their vaccinations and be in close contact with your vet

By ensuring that your cattle are given all their vaccines, you are protecting them from diseases and you are keeping them healthy. Not only that, but you need to think of your cattle as an investment because that's what they are.

By keeping your cattle up-to-date with their vaccines, you're helping to better ensure the protection of your investment. That's why you should create a schedule whereby you will be able to follow up on and stay informed when it comes to new vaccines.

Keep your vet close. Your vet will be able to give you great advice when it comes to your herd and they will be able to notice any early symptoms of diseases in your animals. These are just a few ways whereby you can ensure that your herd is well taken care of.

You are taking care of your herd and learning more about them for the purpose of selling them off in an attempt to make a profit. With this in mind, there are different ways that you can choose to sell off your cattle.

You can decide to sell directly to the butcher, have a sales yard auction, over the hook sales, property sales, feedlot sales, alliances, and forward contracts.

We are going to break down some of these methods and understand their advantages and disadvantages so you can decide for yourself which method you would rather use.

Direct to the butcher/customer

In recent years, there are farmers who have decided to take it upon themselves and reach out to clients directly.

They do not prefer to deal with the middle man and hence they take it upon themselves to reach out to the butchers, restaurants, and other direct clients.

It is a bold move and a lot of people have begun following suit. This method of reaching out has both its positives and negatives.

Advantages

It is the dream of every businessperson to be able to reap the full benefit of their business and to flourish in it. As a business owner, if you are able to get the middle man out of the picture, then it means that you will be able to deal directly with the client and hence you will cut down on the costs that you would have paid to them.

If you are able to make a deal with several butchers and become their main supplier, then you'll be in a great position to do well in business.

You don't have to incur huge costs while transferring cattle since you will only deliver after negotiations with the clients. In some instances, the clients themselves will come to you and hence you get to cut down on costs.

Disadvantages

It is hard to start off if you are not well known and established. If you are new to the business, there are people who have been there before you and they have already established their clientele base.

While starting off, this might take a lot of your time, time that you could have been spending taking care of your cattle since you also have to market your business to find new clients.

Sale yard auction

In a traditional setting during a sale yard auction, cattle would be in the same place and then they would be auctioned one by one. The highest bidder would end up taking the animal.

In the modern setting, the cattle are set aside and placed in an area where they are free from sun or cold weather.

The small sale yard auctions gave way for the regional livestock exchange, which is one of the most preferred methods by both buyers and sellers.

Like any other method, it has its own negatives and positives.

Advantages

With availability of competition and accessibility to a wide range of clients, a regional livestock exchange will attract a large group of people who join together for a common cause.

There are people who are looking for cattle to buy and then there are those who are looking to sell, in this case, the ranchers. People travel far distances so they can acquire the best cattle.

There is competition amongst the buyers and the sellers. Sellers with cattle make an attempt to sell to other buyers.

Buyers then compete to acquire the best bulls and cows.
The cool part about this is that your payment for the livestock sales are guaranteed by the agents who are in charge.

You're also able to set your own prices. You can determine the kind of profit that you would like to make by setting up the price for your cattle.

You can then compare your process with other vendors and see if you are selling at the right price.

Disadvantages

It is an expensive method for selling your herd since there are a lot of costs incurred during the process. You will have to pay the cost for transporting your cattle, weighing them, and you'll have to pay commission fees.

There is a even possibility of collusion between the buyers and the sellers.

You as the person who is going out to sell your cattle at the auction will have to pay the fees involved, regardless of whether or not you actually make a sale.

Forward contracts

This is where a seller and a buyer agree with one another via a contract that the seller will supply the buyer with their product for certain period of time. They also agree on the price that the buyer will be purchasing the product for.

Advantages

The seller will always have a ready market where they will be able to sell their product. This is because of the contracts that they will have with their clients, which will help to give them repeat business.

Disadvantages

The sellers are limited to the agreed upon price that they have with their clients due to the contract that they have made with them.

If a seller were to find a new buyer who would be willing to pay a higher price, the seller might not be able to take advantage of this because of the contract he has with the current client.

Chapter 7: Common Mistakes Even Experienced Ranchers Make that Can Run You Out of Business

Setting up a ranch looks glamorous. In fact, the business can be very profitable if it is handled correctly.

But in order for you to reap the benefits that come with running a ranch and getting to enjoy the profits, you have to be strategic. You have to establish a well-defined plan and structure that will govern how your ranch operates.

If you take time and do a simple search on the web, you will find several cases and testimonials by previous ranch owners who failed to manage their ranch properly. This poor management resulted in them going out of business.

If you are aspiring to set up a ranch, you need to know these common mistakes that beginner ranch owners often make that may result in your venture becoming a failure.

In this chapter, you will learn about some of the top mistakes that even the most experienced ranchers make that may lead to your ranch failing.

1. Failing to plan or failing to update a plan that is out of date

Just as in any business, to run a ranch effectively calls for you to have a plan. In fact, the planning needs for a ranch happen to be more complex than that of a regular business.

Things can get quite complicated if you have possible heirs to the ranch and have no idea how the various assets in the farm will be distributed among them. Also, other than the inheritance plan, failure to have clear operational plans can also be quite costly to you and your ranch business.

Some ranches indeed have a plan but they do not update the plan as things change on the ranch. Failure to update your ranch plan is just as bad as not having a plan in the first place.

When you set up your livestock ranch, ensure you get guidance from someone who is experienced in ranching and draft an effective plan for your ranch.

Bring in the expertise of an attorney, a banker, an accountant, and an insurance specialist.

Together you can draft up a plan for your ranch while at the same time paying keen attention to the wealth and family dynamics in play.

However, it does not stop there. Once you have established a plan, you should ensure that you update it as live events unfold and as policy and law changes are made.

You should always be ready to involve the necessary parties who were originally involved in drafting the initial plan when making any new updates.

2. Going about joint ownership in the wrong manner

There is a widespread notion that owning property, a ranch in this case, in joint names with members of your family is an easy way to plan for a ranch.

Many rely on transfer on death accounts or payable on death accounts and they list their immediate family members as the main beneficiaries when setting up their retirement accounts and life insurance policies. This can be such a huge mistake to make.

While joint ownership helps avoid probate, joint ownership at the same time will increase your chances of losing control over your ranch. Also, joint partnerships, as compared to other types of entities, are not easy to change.
The joint ownership may come with costs and tax implications that are quite significant. Of course not all partnerships are bad.

Partnering with someone who has the right experience can really increase your chances of success. You'll also have someone you can split the costs of the business with.

Really what it all comes down to is making sure that you choose the right partner from the start. Just because someone is related to you, that doesn't mean that person should automatically go into business with you.

Doing something like that can cause you way more problems than benefits.

3. Overlooking liquidity needs

Death and incapacity happen to be quite expensive. There are so many expenses that have to be paid for including family expenses, medical bills, attorney bills, and accountant fees, among others.

In addition to this, federal estate taxes and state death taxes have to be settled as well within a period of nine months after death.

These costs when combined are high. If proper planning is not done, the active managers of the ranch may be forced to sell the ranch or some of the critical equipment required for the ranch at subsidized rates.

As such, it is important that you do not overlook the liquidity needs of your ranch. Assess your liquidity needs and draft an effective repayment plan to help manage your expenses and debts in the event that death or incapacity strikes.

Secure lines of credit, disability insurance, and life insurance to help better protect yourself against these types of things.

4. Assuming ranching is an easy task

Another major mistake you can make is assuming that purchasing the land for your ranch, fencing and getting the livestock on site is all that is needed. This notion has gotten many people in trouble. Ranching is not easy.

Your ranch is your business and you have to acquire enough knowledge of how to run it effectively. This means that you have to invest a lot of your time in reading and acquiring new skills that will help you run your business in a more efficient way.

Those who make this investment and make sacrifices will always thrive. On the other hand, those who overlook this often end up losing a lot of money and possibly having their ranching business collapse.

Before you go into the ranching business, you should know what you are getting yourself into. You should be ready to handle the tough tasks and be ready to learn new things that will be critical to the operations of your ranch.

5. Throwing money at every challenge that pops up in the ranch

Money has the power to cause some massive ground shifts but it may not be the most viable solution for every challenge that comes your way in your ranching business. In fact, you may end up milking your accounts dry in the name of fixing the problems on your ranch.

For instance, if there is a problem with the growth of grass on your ranch, by taking the money approach, you will think the solution is to buy more fertilizer and have new grass planted. The result is that the problem will recur in the future and become more severe.

The best strategy to use when handling the various challenges on the ranch is to understand the root cause of the problem and seek long-term solutions. Maybe the grass in some sections of your ranch is not doing well because your grazing rotations are not effective.

Furthermore, investing in knowledge is key as well. This will help you to better recognize the root cause of a challenge and thus you'll be able to determine what the best solution is.

Sometimes that solution may involve money and other times it may involve changing the way you do things. It is only by taking this approach that you will see returns on your investment.

6. Adding infrastructure to boost profits

Another mistake that people often make is thinking that additional infrastructure will help propel the profits upwards. While a ranch may show great promise of increased revenues, uninformed infrastructure additions may end up being a liability to the ranch.

Before any infrastructure is added, a careful analysis has to be made. Any infrastructural addition should be accompanied with undeniable proof of its necessity and the positive impact the addition would have to the ranch.

The best ranch managers work with the least amount of infrastructure possible. Only the the necessities are set up.

Instead of setting up new structures, you can consider redirecting the money to upgrade and maintain the current infrastructure you have.

You could also train your employees and equip them with a new set of skills that would improve how they operate the ranch. It is simply a matter of making informed decisions for your business.

7. Not getting the right equipment

Make sure that you get the necessary equipment and assets to run your ranch. There are several pieces of equipment that you will need to help you run your ranch effortlessly.

A tractor is useful for hauling hay and feed. You might also need a baler if you are going to plant and harvest your own animal feeds.

Get branding irons to mark your livestock, water troughs to water the animals, feed troughs for feeding the animals and ropes to catch and tie them.

These are some of the common and basic equipment pieces that you will need to acquire.

Having them improves your operations in the ranch thus increasing the value of your ranch.
Without pieces of equipment such as these, day-to-day operations will certainly not be a smooth process.

8. Too big too fast

From a myopic view, it makes sense that the more animals you have in your ranch, the more the profits you will make.
If you are the kind of person who is only driven by the desire to make money fast, then you will quickly get more livestock into your ranch without considering the implications of that action.

If you are wise, you will know that the size of your land, the infrastructure that's in place and the manpower available will dictate the number of livestock that can be accommodated by your ranch.

Instead of focusing on increasing the size of your herd, you should consider ways to increase the productivity of the existing cattle that you have.

Spend your resources ensuring that your animals get quality feeds and the best healthcare.

If the size of your land and the resources available to you can accommodate more animals, you can then consider new breeding practices to improve the quantity of your herd. However, you should never sacrifice quality for quantity. Always make sure that the current cattle you have are well taken care of before trying to increase your numbers.

The rule is not to be blinded by the promise of great profits. Yes, you can increase the number of livestock on your farm. But will the pastures be enough or will the extra animals put more strain on the existing pastures?

Is the water supply sufficient to cater for all the animals on the ranch comfortably?

Can you afford to buy extra feed for your larger herd? The answers to these questions will help you know whether or not to increase the size of your livestock.

9. Poor documentation and record keeping

It is extremely important to store all the documents and records for your ranch in a secure place. Only the people in charge of handling the records should be able to access them.

Some of the important records to keep are the title deed for the land, tax returns and the plans for the ranch business. These documents are extremely important when dealing with the government or insurance companies.

You should strive to keep a record of every transaction that happens in your ranch. Your accounting books should be updated with every detail of income and expenditure. This will help you easily track the performance of your ranch.

10. Failure to get an insurance cover

There is a lot of uncertainty that one is faced with when running a ranch. An accident or a natural calamity can occur resulting in loss of your assets. This is where insurance comes in handy.

Insurance is a way of shielding you from losing everything you have invested your resources in. Even with the knowledge of the importance of ranch insurance, some ranch owners still go ahead and run their ranches without insurance.

This often proves to be a costly mistake in the long-run. As such, if you are a ranch owner, you should consider getting insurance for your ranch. Get the best policy that covers everything and everyone that is involved in the running of your ranch.

This gives you the assurance that in the event of a calamity, you will receive compensation for the losses incurred.

You do not always have to learn things the hard way. You can always learn from the mistakes and the experiences that other people have gone through.

Ensure that you do not commit the mistakes listed above in this section. If you do, then you will risk watching your investment sink.

Conclusion

Thank you for taking the time to read his book and I hope that it has helped you in one way or another. This is an easy guide on how to become a rancher and with the basics down, you can pursue ranching as a lifestyle.

It is difficult to get started on any business venture and ranching is no exception. However, if you develop an interest and enjoy what you do then it certainly makes things easier.

You want to ensure that as a rancher you are steps ahead when it comes to the feeds that you will give to your cattle, their health, their market value and emerging trends. One of the main keys to being a successful rancher is to be continually learning.

You should carry out constant research and remain informed as often as you can.

Seek out expert opinions and carry out a lot of research before you get started. Look at the successful ranchers and see what they are doing.

Finally, if this book was helpful to you in any way, please leave a positive review. It would be greatly appreciated and it'll help others know if the book is right for them.
Thank you!

www.ingramcontent.com/pod-product-compliance
Lightning Source LLC
Chambersburg PA
CBHW030018190526
45157CB00016B/3130